INNOVATIVE
SOY COOKING

TRUDIE BURNHAM

THE CROSSING PRESS SPECIALTY COOKBOOKS

THE CROSSING PRESS **FREEDOM, CALIFORNIA**

For information on bulk purchases or group discounts for this and other Crossing Press titles, please contact our Special Sales Manager at 800-777-1048.

Visit our Website on the Internet at: www.crossingpress.com

Library of Congress Cataloging-in-Publication Data

Burnham, Trudie.
    Innovative soy cooking / by Trudie Burnham.
        p. cm. -- (Specialty cookbooks)
    Includes index.
    ISBN 0-89594-962-8 (pbk.)
    1. Cookery (Soybeans) 2. Soyfoods I. Title.
    II. Series: Crossing Press specialty cookbooks.
    TX803.S6B87   1998
    641.6'5655--dc21
                                        98-26030
                                        CIP

CONTENTS

I thank Margaret Kirkwood, this book's first typist, for her input and encouragement. If this book is my brainchild, Margie was certainly its midwife.

PREFACE

My cooking style is dreadfully undisciplined. I work spontaneously with whatever ingredients are on hand, and nothing is measured. This was a big drawback when I worked as a research and development person in a soy dairy. I'd come up with great-tasting things, but no recipe. I wanted to see how closely I could simulate a popular dish using soy products instead of animal foods and still have a palatable result. The surprise was that many of the new products actually tasted better, felt lighter in the stomach, and were preferred by the consumers. I hope you will like these recipes.

Most recipes here will feed four. If there is a variation, I'll mention it and also supply advice about shelf life.

INTRODUCTION

Let's face it. In a society like ours, obsessed with fast, low-fat food, tofu is the ultimate answer. The cooking is all done before it gets to you. You can even eat it straight from the pack, cubed and doused with tamari as the Japanese do in hot weather. It is the ideal food for busy folk who want a meal on the table within a half hour. Besides providing clean, high-quality, cholesterol-free protein, soybeans are iron-rich, estrogen-enhancing, and, for most people, easy to digest.

In short, I've written a user-friendly guide to a soya-based vegetarian diet. You will find that the recipes span a range of ethnic ingredients and dishes. This book may appeal to the newly initiated or the to old hand looking for a few fresh ideas. Many recipes are vegan, or employ a minimum of dairy food. I suspect that many people who are switching to vegetarian diets tend to substitute dairy products for animal proteins, and discover that the resulting congestion is not conducive to good health. Here are clues for you to develop an eating style that minimizes the consumption of processed foods, but maximizes your time. And that's before we even get to the health benefits.

I am up to a surreptitious food revolution in this book, but I do not want to promote a kind of New Age Puritanism where we can't allow ourselves the rich foods people have come to enjoy. However, I think that some things should be eaten in moderation, meat and dairy for instance. I want to show anyone who seeks a lighter, life-force-filled diet that it is possible to make great dishes with soy products. Such food can be sensuously, delightfully pleasing to the palate and the eye. Yes, tofu wakame lasagne can be enjoyed with a full-bodied Beaujolais.

I felt I'd really pulled a coup de cuisine the night I served my unsuspecting mother a lasagne made with tofu and seaweed and was highly praised for the dish. I knew then that if I could pull one over on my Midwestern mom, that I must be developing a talent of some kind in the food alchemy field.

I like to buy foods and store them in glass jars on open shelves. Not all the items are immediately recognizable to the untrained eye. "What do you do with all this strange stuff?" people ask. I begin to explain that most of them are soybean products and a few of their extended family members. The penny drops. "Ah!" they say, suspecting I have allergies, "You eat this stuff because you have to." "No," I reply, beaming, "I eat it because I like it."

There's no denying that more and more items are landing on the grocer's shelves that look as though they may have been delivered by a flying saucer. I could launch into a description of food combining, vegetarian theory, and the wholesomeness of whole grain diets and foods from the Far East, but why alienate you? The central premise of my food philosophy is not radical: Food that is good for you should taste the best.

If we start with fresh, high-quality ingredients and apply a modicum of technique to preserve that quality when we prepare them, we should end up with appealing, healthy food. If we go to the trouble to secure foods that are fresh, uncanned, unprocessed, and unrefined, our delight in our diets should increase. If you have been exposed to bland, boring, or rancid "health foods," please keep on reading.

I encourage you to eliminate some food items you won't see in my recipes: margarine (because of the hydrogenation), meat, refined oils, white flours, white sugars, and commercial salt. I'd suggest you use these foods in moderation: dairy (milk, cheese, butter, yogurt, cream), fried foods, eggs, and flour. You may have to change your marketing habits to find some of the ingredients used in this book. Look for a whole foods store that sells stuff in bulk. It might cost a bit more, but I think you'll find it is worth the extra cents in terms of freshness and quality. *Never* hesitate to return anything your nose does not endorse, wherever you shop. Rancid oils or oil-bearing items (nuts, flours, wheat germ, and the like) are very hard on the liver and your nose knows!

In my more uppity phases, I don't buy unless I can (1) smell it on the spot (especially shelled nuts), and (2) sprout it. Food that hasn't enough life-force left to sprout and re-create itself is too old to eat or has possibly been irradiated. This applies to all beans, grains (uncracked), legumes, and seeds (unhusked).

Remember, if something has been cut off from nature's original packaging, it is starting to decay from the moment that happens.

The body is not only a machine that extracts energy from fuel, it is a home for a living spirit that is fed by the life-force inherent in foods that grow from the earth. The more life-force in your food, the healthier you are in spirit. The less life-force your body receives, the more rapidly it starts to decay and the spirit becomes pale. This is why I strongly advocate sprouting everything in sight. Start with alfalfa sprouts as they are the easiest for the uninitiated. Don't bother with the anemic, plastic-imprisoned sprouts you see in most stores. For a few cents worth of seed, you can get your own garden going on the kitchen counter with the simple setup of a glass jar and a piece of nylon screen.

Ingredients

Here is my ingredients list.

Kelp: I am referring to dried, granulated kelp. It can be measured by the teaspoon or sprinkled like a condiment, depending on your fondness for saltiness. There is no need to get too particular about the brand or country it's from. And you can decide whether you want a coarse or fine ground—a fine grind is better for sauces.

Kudzu: This is a cornstarch-like substance made from a root. It comes in dried white chunks, which dissolve easily in water. I prefer to use it instead of cornstarch and other thickeners, which have little nutritional value.

Lecithin: This comes in two forms, liquid and granular. The liquid type is very viscous and messy to measure by the teaspoon (I just eyeball it). You may prefer the granular type for this reason. In items with a more liquid texture, like dressings, the liquid sort is preferable, but the granular form, if dissolved, will work as well.

Mirin: This has a very distinct flavor. You may recognize it as the flavoring in sushi rice. It's a fermented liquid similar to vinegar. Once you have a bottle on hand, experiment with it. I find it very useful in sauces, dressings, and stir-fries.

Miso: This fermented product comes in many varieties. Japanese miso is made of soybeans, salt, a rice starter, and, occasionally, additional grains. Do some tasting and find the type that suits your palate. Here are three types: mugi, a soft, dark, medium flavor; hatcho, a rich, strong, well-aged variety (sort of the cabernet sauvignon of misos); and brown rice, in the middle of the road. American-made misos are very good these days: Cold Mountain comes readily to mind, with white and yellow misos that are sweeter and lighter, which some people prefer. In some recipes I specify the type of miso, in others try the kind you like best. One or two recipes call for natto miso, which is a pickled barley chutney-style affair.

Nutritional Yeast: This is the dried, golden yellow powder or flake-style yeast, which usually has some salt added. You may find it in bins at the health food store. It is entirely different from yeast which is used to raise breads and cakes.

Oils: In this book I want to concentrate on ways to make our diets better and to encourage positive changes in eating habits. I don't use lard and bacon grease, as these concentrated fats contain toxins and chemicals; all rendered fats are rancid, carcinogenic, and indigestible. They should not be consumed.

Cottonseed and some other oils such as nonorganic flax seed and palm kernel oils are not foodstuffs and hence are not governed by regulations concerning purity (pesticides are used freely on these products). A few rungs up the ladder are safflower, peanut, olive, and soybean oil that have been extracted from their source with chemicals or heat, both negative in their effects. Also antioxidants (to prevent the oil from getting rancid on the shelf) are added to these oils…more chemicals.

The oils you should use are expeller pressed or cold pressed (no heat or chemicals involved), oils from seeds (sunflower, sesame), from nuts (almond, walnut), from vegetables (olive and peanut), and a few others for specialty items—wheat germ, coconut, apricot kernel, pumpkin seed, and linseed oil.

Longevity researchers are finding that free radicals are a major cause of cell degeneration. All oils bear and release these free radicals as they are breaking down and decaying. This decay is hastened by frying and the heat-extraction process. Only peanut and olive oil should be used for frying as these are the least affected by this process. Throw any oil out once it has been used.

Natural oils come in different degrees of purity or refinement. Many will cloud if you refrigerate them or have a precipitated solid matter at the bottom. Thicker oils go well in some recipes, while the more refined or lighter ones work better in others. Where I have not indicated a specific oil, use your favorite from my recommendations above.

Sea Vegetables: There are endless kinds of edible seaweed (in fact, most are edible), so I will list those that appear in this book, mostly by their Japanese names because that's how you will find them at the market: agar-agar, which comes in clear sticks and is used in many dishes as a generic thickener (it's a good vegetarian gelatin replacement); arame, a flattish, thready-looking seaweed, mostly black; dulse (also known as karengo), a reddish brown type with a dried leaf sort of appearance (it becomes extremely tender when soaked and is the mildest flavored of the lot); hijiki, also black, looks like snarled-up bits of yarn or little twigs; kombu, purchased in long leathery-looking strips, needs a good soaking or boiling to limber up (not for the uninitiated as it tends to retain its rubbery texture); nori, flat black or green sheets of seaweed (most people recognize it as sushi wrapping); sea farine, very similar to agar-agar, is also used as a thickener, though it has a smoother texture and comes in a shreddy coarse powder;

wakame, also in strips but feathery and more delicate than kombu.

Seeds: All kinds are used in this book. Sunflower, pumpkin, poppy, and sesame are for eating; alfalfa, radish, red clover, and fenugreek are for sprouting.

Shitake: These dried forest mushrooms are commonly sold in most Asian stores. They are currently in favor in gourmet circles and can also be found fresh. If you turn into a big fan, you can even get yourself a small "grow-it-at-home" log with the little fungi friends sprouting out.

Slippery Elm Powder: Made from the finely ground bark of the slippery elm tree, this powder has a mild sweet flavor and pronounced thickening abilities.

Soy Milk: This beverage is available almost everywhere now in a long-life pasteurized form. At soy dairies or Asian markets you can find a fresh product, though it may be hard to find it unsugared at the latter. It is milk expressed from cooked soybeans.

In its powdered form, it tastes nasty, a bit like chalk in suspension. Do yourself a favor. When you are next in your favorite health food store, try a drink of fresh unsugared soy milk. It's a whole different animal to that powdered stuff.

Soy milk boasts no animal fats or cholesterol and is very high in iron and protein. It blends masterfully with sesame (tahini and sesame oil) and the milder seaweeds (agar-agar and sea farine), and has an uncanny affinity for slippery elm. If you ever need to make soy milk thick, creamy, and defiantly nondairy-rich, try the old slippery elm.

Soy milk has received some bad press because of its gas-producing qualities. The main cause is the addition of that old devil, white sugar, for flavoring, which causes the milk to ferment during the digestion process. I know two ways to avoid the gas: (1) never drink sugared soy milk. If you are really sensitive, acquire a taste for the unsweetened (no honey even) variety. I inhaled almost a quart of this a day while pregnant and my hair and fingernails grew at an unreal pace! and (2) drink soy milk prepared from sprouted soybeans. The sprouting breaks down the digestive inhibitor (which explains why dried soybeans must be well boiled) and greatly increases its food potential.

Encourage your local soy dairy to try sprouted beans, or make your own soy milk.

Soy sauce: Like miso, true shoyu, or tamari, is a fermented product made from soybeans and salt. The name implies a tradition of careful preparation. It has a rich, savory, quite distinctive flavor. It is lots more expensive than ordinary soy sauce and may be a refinement you want to adopt only if your palate is discriminating. Otherwise a more generic product will suffice.

Soysage: This mock sausage product, originally invented at The Farm in Tennessee, is now re-created by many soycrafters as a soy deli item.

Sweeteners: When soybeans and sweets or fruits are mixed in some desserts and drinks, gas sometimes results. Experiment by trying out each dessert by itself, not after a heavy protein meal, to see how your body responds. I find that combining lecithin, carminative seeds (fennel, anise, cumin, dill, caraway, and cardamom), or some of the slower burning nuts and seeds with the sweetener will mitigate fermentation considerably. Even so, our favorite nightcap during the soy parlor days was a slightly warmed glass of soymilk with a spoonful of molasses stirred in it.

I try not to use refined sugar in any form, brown, white, or turbinado. If it's crystallized, it is refined. I generally bake and cook with a mild-flavored, unfiltered honey. I use malt syrup when I want a crispier texture in baking, or a caramel taste.

In sweet treats or snacks, molasses is acceptable but always bear in mind that it is a sugar cane product and may have been raised under some fairly noxious conditions (in Hawaii, for example, 2-4D, paraquat, and other defoliants are routinely sprayed over the fields). Grill your purveyors for a profile of their products. Select an organic product if it exists.

Date sugar (dried, crystallized dates pulverized into grains) is a good sweetener. Raisin butter is a great sweetener in baking, if you happen to be low on honey, as I was one day. Soak raisins or sultanas (you could also use currants) overnight covered in water. Drain the fruit and whirl in a blender until smooth like butter.

Used in breads or cookies this fruit butter adds an interesting citric or sourish flavor and helps to keep baked goods moist for a long time. Carob, oatmeal, or tahini cookies taste much richer with this addition. Use the same quantity as honey. Rice malt syrup is another good sweetener but I find it expensive and therefore reserve it for candies and toffees and special confections.

Tahini: This is a paste made of ground roasted or raw sesame seeds, either hulled or unhulled. It is available almost everywhere now.

Tempeh: This product is made of semicooked soybeans inoculated with a mushroom-like culture. It comes as a flat cake and is generally sliced thin and fried or steamed. Unlike tofu, it is not a table-ready product and requires further cooking. Tempeh with many different additions is now available, and any type is suitable in these recipes.

Tofu: This is the cheese made by coagulating soy milk and pressing the resultant curds in settling boxes. It comes in many styles with varying texture and water content. Many groceries now offer a choice of tofu in increasing stages of firmness: silken, soft, and firm. Silken tofu, having been sieved through an extremely fine mesh, is the most creamy in texture and is excellent for thickening soups and for making desserts and mayonnaise. The soft is good for scrambling, as well as in some dips and spreads. Firm tofu is best for teriyaki cutlets for barbecuing.

Umeboshi Plums: Here is another traditional Japanese food, made of salted plums seasoned with beefsteak leaves. They are dark pink, olive-sized, unpitted plums. It is also available in paste form, with no pips.

Vinegars: Unless otherwise indicated, use *organic* apple cider vinegar if at all possible. Other vinegars used are rice wine vinegar or herbed white wine vinegar.

Utensils and Techniques

Probably the most expensive suggestion I have for you is this: go into your kitchen, take out all your aluminum cookware and utensils, and throw them out. I can save you a lot of time reading scientific literature and assure you that cooking in aluminum pots and pans can contribute to chronic kidney malfunction and Alzheimer's disease. Buying organic foods makes no sense if their fate is to be prepared in aluminum cookware. I know I promised not to get too purist, but anything is better than aluminum, so get rid of it now.

A strainer/colander lined with a piece of cheesecloth is useful for draining tofu. A blender is helpful. A food processor not essential but a great time-saver. From the Asian market a few items come in handy—a suribachi (a Japanese mortar and pestle), a bamboo rolling mat, a ginger grater (which works for nutmeg and Parmesan too). I also recommend changing your salt and pepper shakers over to granulated kelp and garlic shakers respectively. (Give the sodium silico-aluminate salt to the kids for making play dough.) A rolling pin is needed for some pastries, although I have used a wine bottle in a pinch.

To press tofu into steaks, cut an average firm block into four slabs, one inch thick. Place on waxed paper (the tofu will absorb flavors from wood) between two cutting boards and press with a weight, such as a heavy pan filled with water. Let stand somewhere that the excess liquid can drain for two to three hours. The result should be a firm tofu cutlet one-half-inch thick.

To press soft tofu, line a sieve or colander with cheesecloth or a smooth dish towel. Break the tofu cake and crumble it into the cloth. Squeeze it and let stand for an hour or so. Place a bowl or small plate on top and weigh it down. The tofu should have the consistency of cottage cheese.

APPETIZERS, SNACKS, AND SIDE ORDERS

These recipes have the virtue of being quick to fix (10 minutes). Most will keep well over a week or so. They also travel well and, like all soy foods, digest slowly and evenly, giving extended energy during the day. Quite a few can be spread on breads and crackers and can double as dips or hors d'oeuvres on short notice.

Tofu Dip

Here come soybeans at the cocktail hour! This party-goer could be made a day earlier as it improves while it sits.

The Two-Minute Dip

Cream 1 pound tofu until smooth and add the contents of an organic instant onion soup package. Blend thoroughly.

The Ten-Minute Dip

1 pound (1 block) tofu
½ onion, diced
1 clove garlic, crushed or minced
¼ cup blue cheese (or shredded cheddar or cream Neufchâtel)
¼ teaspoon celery seed
1 tablespoon soy sauce
3 tablespoons poppy seeds
1 tablespoon apple cider vinegar
Chopped walnuts (optional)

Cream the tofu until smooth, add the remaining ingredients (except the walnuts), and blend thoroughly. Sprinkle some chopped walnuts on top, if desired.

The Indian Dip

1 pound tofu (1 block)
1 teaspoon curry powder
1 tablespoon apple cider vinegar *or* lemon juice
1 tablespoon soy sauce
¼ cup chopped green onion
Dash toasted sesame oil
½ teaspoon honey
½ teaspoon mustard powder
Minced chives (or green onion tops minced)

Cream the tofu until smooth, blend in the remaining ingredients (except the chives). Sprinkle the chives on top.

MISSING EGG SALAD

I invented this and word seemed to travel fast and wide, because I saw it in a California deli a year later, with the same name.

1 cup mashed, drained tofu
¼ cup very dry pressed tofu, cut into strips or slivered
¼ cup Tofu Mayonnaise (page 37)
¼ cup chopped celery
¼ onion, diced
1 teaspoon garlic powder
1 teaspoon kelp
½ teaspoon turmeric powder
1 ½ teaspoons dill weed
2 tablespoons poppy seeds
2 tablespoons diced pickles (dill and/or sweet)
2 tablespoons sunflower seeds
2 tablespoons soy sauce (to taste)
1 tablespoon apple cider vinegar
1 tablespoon smooth mustard

Mash the tofu with the mayonnaise. Add the remaining ingredients, taste, and adjust seasoning. Let sit for a while to mingle. Spread on fresh whole wheat bread, add a handful of alfalfa sprouts, and munch!

If you are making this for the next day, throw in a handful of dried lentils (washed); they'll soften overnight, add crunch, and absorb excess moisture.

Preparation time: 10–12 minutes

Tofu Avocado Spread

1 cup pressed crumbled tofu
1 avocado, mashed
2 tablespoons lime juice (squeezed over
    avocado)
2 tablespoons white or yellow miso (or
    natto for stronger flavor)
1 teaspoon soy sauce

½ teaspoon kelp
½ teaspoon granulated garlic
1 tablespoon nutritional yeast (optional)

Cream together and use as spread.

Preparation time: 10 minutes

PIGLESS PÂTÉ

This and the following spreads are great on rice crackers or rye crisp as hors d'oeuvres or quick lunches.

You need to have ready access to some kind of soysage to make this recipe. To make soysage yourself is a pain! Or you could try a veggie burger with the right moist consistency, provided it doesn't require further cooking.

½ **cup soysage**
½ **cup drained tofu**
2 **tablespoons miso (mugi or brown rice)**
½ **teaspoon toasted sesame oil**
1 **teaspoon soy sauce**
1 **teaspoon garlic granules**
3 **tablespoons minced green or red onion**

1 **tablespoon nutritional yeast**
3 **dill pickles, diced**

Cream the soysage and tofu. Add the miso and cream again. Then add oil, soy sauce, garlic, onion, and yeast. Stir into a cohesive paste and add the pickles at the end.

Suggestion

- For those who like their lilies gilded, try hollowing a block of firm tofu, fill it with pâté, and chill. Marinate it in a combination of 2 teaspoons soy sauce, 1 teaspoon kelp, 2 teaspoons rubbed sage, and top with sliced green olives.

Preparation time: 5 minutes

TASTY CHEDDAR/WALNUT TOFU SPREAD

These spreads are great wrapped in a crisp lettuce leaf or on your usual sandwich bread.

1 cup mashed tofu
½ cup shredded sharp cheddar
½ teaspoon each kelp and garlic granules
2 teaspoons soy sauce (if cheese is not salty enough)
½–⅓ cup tofu or regular mayonnaise
¼ cup chopped walnuts
¼ cup chopped green onion
¼ cup chopped celery
2 tablespoons sunflower seeds

Mash the tofu and cheese together. Stir in the spices, soy sauce, and mayonnaise, and cream together. Add the chopped ingredients and sunflower seeds. The result should be a smooth sandwich spread with some crunch.

Preparation time: 10 minutes

TOFU YEAST TAHINI SPREAD

1 cup mashed tofu
3 tablespoons tahini
2 tablespoons miso (mugi or natto)
2 teaspoons each kelp and garlic granules
1 teaspoon lemon juice
2 tablespoons nutritional yeast
1 tablespoon sunflower seeds

The technique here is to mash the tofu, cream in the tahini, then the miso, then the spices, lemon juice, yeast, and sunflower seeds. Stir thoroughly. This keeps well in the fridge for lunches or to add to a green salad.

Preparation time: 10 minutes

Miso Tahini Spread

⅓ **cup miso (brown rice variety is good)**
⅓ **cup tahini**
2 or 3 green onions, chopped
Kelp and garlic powder to taste

Cream together and spread. This is excellent on toast with avocado or makes a great sandwich with tomato, sprouts, avocado, and Tofu Mayonnaise (page 37).

Preparation time: 5 minutes

Nori Rolls ala Ume

Allow yourself 1 hour and 20 minutes to boil the grains for this seaweed classic. This dish takes some preparation time (25 minutes) but keeps well for many days in the refrigerator as long as it's kept dry. A slatted bamboo roller is a help here and also makes a good dish cover. Toasting the nori peps up the moist seaweed and makes the sheets easy to work with.

1 to 1 ½ cups dry grains, such as ⅓ brown rice or mochi (sweet brown rice), ⅓ husked (uncracked) wheat, ⅓ husked (uncracked) rye kernels (adzuki beans make a good variant)
1 cup chopped Chinese veggies (½ cup carrots or broccoli; green beans; ½ cup onions and crumbled seasoned tofu)
2–3 tablespoons oil
8–10 sheets of nori
8–10 chopped umeboshi plums

Cook the grains in water, usually 2 cups water to 1 cup of grain. Sauté the vegetables in the oil with a dash of soy sauce, kelp, and garlic for flavor. Set aside.

Toast the nori over an open flame (electric coils will also work) until the color changes subtly from black to green. Lay the nori out flat (on a bamboo roller if you have one). On one end, spread one layer of grains, a thin strip of tofu and veggies, and an even thinner strip of the chopped umeboshi plums (as a condiment).

Some may like to use tuna flakes here in traditional Japanese style. Place more grains on top and roll. The recalcitrant nori will stick to itself if you moisten the end (like a rolling paper). Let it stand on its sealed edge as you complete the process.

Makes 6 to 8 rolls. They're great cold, and can be wrapped whole for lunches, or sliced about ¾ -inch thick for hors d'oeuvres or snacks.

Preparation time: 25 minutes; 80 minutes to boil grains

Lentil Sprout Liverwurst

This is better than liverwurst. Liver and lentil sprouts have two things in common. They're remarkably high in choline, an essential amino acid, and they have a very distinctive taste. For those of you who have cultivated a fondness for liverwurst and have reluctantly left this food behind, here is something to look forward to.

2 cups lentil sprouts
⅓ cup nutritional yeast
3 teaspoons soy sauce
¼ cup sesame or olive oil
¼ cup tahini, sunflower seed butter, cashew butter, or peanut butter
½ sweet onion, chunked

Sprout the lentils by soaking them overnight in water. Use a 2-quart jar with a nylon screen square on top secured with a rubber band. Drain them well and rinse daily. They'll be ready for use on the second and third day.

Put all ingredients in a food processor and whiz until creamed. If you don't have a food processor but have a suribachi (a Japanese mortar and pestle), put the lentil sprouts in the suribachi first, then place the other ingredients in a bowl and blend well. Chill. Some people like to add a green flavor like chopped parsley or fresh basil leaves.

Preparation time: 10–12 minutes; 30 minutes to chill

Mermaid Marinade

This dish is a mineralized munch! The two best sea-weeds for it are kombu and wakame. It's very light in weight, but assume that a quart jar will take 20 to 30 six-inch strips.

Wakame or kombu
1 onion, sliced in rings
10 to 12 cloves of garlic (as many as you will eat)
Beefsteak leaves from umeboshi plums
Sprigs of dill
½ cup sesame or olive oil
½ cup rice wine vinegar or herbed white vinegar
2 tablespoons soy sauce
2 teaspoons mirin

Soak the seaweed for about 30 minutes to remove excess salt (and little crustacean hitch-hikers). Drain well and cut into manageable pieces, about six inches long. In a canning jar, coil the seaweed and layer it with the onion rings, garlic, and the beefsteak leaves from your umeboshi plums, if you're so inspired. Put some dill in too if you like the flavor. Make a dressing of the remaining ingredients. Pour over the seaweed and seal the jar. Give it a few days to let the flavors mingle. This makes an excellent condiment for rice or a nice addition to a fresh green salad. It will keep for a month or more stored in the fridge.

Preparation time: 10 minutes; 30 minutes to soak the seaweed

SEED YOGURT

Allow time for the seeds to soak overnight.

½ **cup sesame seeds**
½ **cup sunflower seeds**
¼ **cup raisins, currants, sultanas, chopped dates, figs, dried apricots**
¼ **cup almonds**
⅛ **cup cashews**
⅓ **cup flaked coconut**
⅛ **cup flax seed (linseed)**
2 **cups cool water**

Soak the seeds and remaining ingredients for 10 to 12 hours in the water.

Grind in the blender and refrigerate the mixture as it is best chilled. Add cinnamon, allspice, nutmeg, cardamom, or honey to taste if you like variation.

This mix lasts about 7 to 10 days refrigerated. It gets a sour snap, then outright ferments. Some prefer it with more seeds.

Suggestions

- Try a scoop in half a papaya.
- Top off your fruit salad.
- Add to cooked oatmeal as a sweetener.
- Mix with dry oats and grated apple, squeeze an orange over all, and combine—delicious!

Preparation time: 5 minutes

YEASTY POPCORN

This seriously underrated snack food can be served in a savory style without salt and melted butter, two ingredients that really defeat its health value. Technique is everything when it comes to popping corn at home. A cast iron pan works best for good, even heat. Heat the pan and cover the bottom with olive oil (about 1 1/2 tablespoons for 8-inch diameter). Add popcorn (about 1/4 cup) to cover the bottom in one layer. Cover the pan and shake it often until popping starts. Keep it on the heat, letting steam out periodically until popping stops. Shake again and be careful not to burn the kernels at the end.

4 cups popped popcorn
1 to 1 ½ teaspoons soy sauce or kecap (Indonesian sweetened soy sauce)
2 tablespoons savory nutritional yeast
½ teaspoon granulated garlic
½ teaspoon kelp
Pinch cayenne pepper (if you like it hot)
½ teaspoon Spike

Drip the soy sauce over the popped popcorn, mix the remaining ingredients, and sprinkle over. Make lots—it goes fast.

Preparation time: 8 minutes

MARINATED TOFU SALAD

Prepare one of the following marinades.

Herb Marinade

¼ cup light oil
¼ cup herbal tarragon or dill vinegar *or*
   lemon/lime juice
2 fresh garlic cloves, pressed
Some chopped onion if it's handy
½ teaspoon dried oregano
½ teaspoon dried thyme
½ teaspoon dried marjoram

Blend all the ingredients in a nonreactive bowl. Instead of the three herbs, you can substitute 1 teaspoon dried dill.

Teriyaki Marinade

⅓ cup soy sauce
Juice of 1 lime
1 tablespoon sesame seeds
1 teaspoon toasted sesame oil
1 teaspoon honey
1 teaspoon kelp
3 fresh garlic cloves, pressed
Thumbnail of ginger, pressed

Blend all the ingredients in a nonreactive bowl and add the tofu.

1 block tofu, dry pressed, thinly sliced
1 medium-size head romaine lettuce,
   drained, and torn
2 large tomatoes chopped or ½ cup cherry
   tomatoes
3 or 4 green onions, sliced
Fresh mushrooms, sliced
Alfalfa sprouts

Toss the vegetables and then add the slices of tofu. Use one of the above marinades as a salad dressing.

Suggestions

- Instead of the Herb Marinade, you can use Umeboshi Dressing (page 43).
- Instead of the Teriyaki Marinade, you can use Shabu-Shabu (page 42).
- You can also simply place the sliced tofu in one of the marinades and eat it that way, drained. It will keep in the refrigerator for 2 to 3 weeks.

Unpeeled Potato Salad

10 small/medium potatoes, washed, cubed, boiled in skins, and cooled
2 stalks celery, diced
1 large sweet onion, diced
40–50 black or green olives, sliced
4 hard-boiled eggs, chopped (optional)
2 large dill pickles, diced

Dressing

1 cup Tofu Mayonnaise (page 37)
½ cup sour cream (optional) or you can substitute soy yogurt, yogurt, or thick soy milk
2 tablespoons mild or whole grain mustard
2 teaspoons soy sauce
4 sprigs parsley, chopped
1 teaspoon kelp
½ teaspoon celery seed
½ teaspoon crushed garlic
1 ½ tablespoons honey (optional)
3 tablespoons lemon juice *or* 2 tablespoons apple cider vinegar

Cut the potatoes into bite-sized hunks and place in a large bowl. Add the remaining ingredients (except the dressing) and toss.

In another bowl, cream the mayonnaise with the sour cream and mustard. Add the soy sauce, parsley, seasonings, and honey, if desired, with the lemon juice, and stir till blended. Add the dressing to the vegetables, stir evenly through, and chill. This salad is great on the second day, but how hard it is to wait!

Preparation time: 20 minutes; 25 minutes to boil the potatoes

Peanut Butter/Sprout Salad

This may not sound edible to you, but it's a great protein snack and can satisfy hunger for hours on the run. Oh, it does taste good too, if you like peanut butter.

2 tablespoons butter or olive oil or half of each
⅓ cup peanut butter
¼ cup water
Dash kelp and garlic

Big handful of soybean and/or mung sprouts, chilled and crisp
Lemon juice

Warm the first four ingredients until the butter melts, stir until blended, cool slightly.

Rinse the sprouts and put them in a large bowl. Squirt lemon juice over them and then pour the peanut sauce over the top. Toss and serve.

Preparation time: 5 minutes

Gado Gado

3 potatoes, cut into large cubes, about 2 cups

⅓ head cabbage, sliced, about 2 cups

1 cup soy sprouts

1 block tofu

4 ounces tempeh

2 tablespoons olive oil or butter

½ cup roasted peanuts and water whirled in blender or ⅓ cup peanut butter

½ teaspoon soy sauce

1 tablespoon lemon juice

2 cloves garlic, minced

½ tablespoon kelp

¼ teaspoon chili powder (if you like it spicy)

⅓ cup white wine *or* 3 teaspoons lemon juice

½–1 cup brown rice balls (if you have left-over brown rice stuck together in clumps so much the better)

Boil or steam the potatoes and cabbage till soft; add the sprouts at the last minute. Set aside to cool.

Cut the tofu and tempeh into cubes or strips, pan-fry in a little olive oil, drain, and set aside.

Warm the oil (or butter), add the peanuts and soy sauce, and blend. Stir in the lemon juice, garlic, kelp, and chili powder, if desired. Simmer a while and at the end add the wine or lemon juice, cooking until blended.

Arrange the cooled veggies, rice, tofu, and tempeh on a platter and ladle the sauce over the top.

Suggestion

- This dish can be a whole meal. You can also serve it with just the sprouts, veggies, and sauce as a prelude to, say, tofu curry.

Preparation time: 25 minutes

DULSE (OR KARENGO) TABOULI

Here is a cold grain salad, good for summer fare.

1 cup bulgur wheat
1 ½ cups cold water
1 handful of dulse
2 tomatoes, chopped in chunks
1 onion, diced
8–10 mint leaves (if available), chopped
5–6 sprigs parsley, minced
1–2 cloves garlic (optional)

Soak the bulgur in the water until it is moist and fluffy. In another bowl, soak the dulse until soft. Drain off the excess water. Mix everything together and stir. Add pressed garlic (1 or 2 cloves) if you like it spicy. Season the salad with apple cider vinegar, olive oil, and soy sauce, or try Umeboshi Dressing (page 43), omitting the dill.

Preparation time: 30 minutes to soak bulgar, 5 minutes to mix

Tofu Mayonnaise

6–8 ounces tofu, cut into chunks
1 tablespoon soy sauce
2 tablespoons lemon juice
¼ cup apple cider vinegar
2 tablespoons honey
½ teaspoon garlic powder
½ teaspoon lecithin
2–3 tablespoons oil (light sesame oil or wheat germ oil for interesting taste)

Whirl the tofu in a blender until smooth (like cream cheese); add the soy sauce, lemon juice, vinegar, and honey, and blend again. If your brand of tofu is too moist for good consistency, try a little lecithin to set it or next time press some water out before blending.

Preparation time: 8 minutes

MISSING EGG MEDITERRANEAN MAYONNAISE

Spicier than Tofu Mayonnaise, this is good on veggies, especially artichokes.

6–8 ounces tofu (soft or silken)
¼ cup lemon juice
2 cloves garlic, pressed
½ teaspoon kelp
1 tablespoon soy sauce
½ teaspoon lecithin
3 tablespoons olive oil

1 tablespoon coarse grain mustard (optional)

Blend the tofu, add the lemon juice, garlic, kelp, soy sauce, and lecithin. Blend again. While the mixture is whizzing, dribble in the olive oil until you have the appropriate consistency. Add the mustard for a real zing.

Preparation time: 8 minutes

BLUE CHEESE DRESSING

½ **pound tofu**
⅛ **cup oil**
1 **tablespoon apple cider vinegar** *or* **lemon juice**
½ **teaspoon kelp**
1 **clove garlic, pressed**
¼ **wedge sweet white onion (omit if too sharp)**
¼ **pound blue cheese, crumbled**

In a blender, whirl the tofu until creamy. Dribble in the oil and vinegar, then add the kelp, pressed garlic, and onion. Throw the cheese in last and blend lightly if you like it chunky. The cheese should make the dressing salty enough for you, but add a dash of soy sauce if it seems too bland. It is best to let the dressing stand for an hour or so to allow the flavors to mellow.

Suggestion

● About ¼ teaspoon of celery seed added while blending gives an interesting texture and goes nicely with the other flavors.

Preparation time: 6 minutes

TOFU AVOCADO GODDESS DRESSING

½ cup crumbled silken tofu
½ cup mashed avocado (1 small or ½ large)
3 tablespoons lime or lemon juice
⅛ cup oil (optional, especially if avocados are rich)
1 tablespoon soy sauce
½ teaspoon kelp
1 garlic clove, pressed
½ teaspoon dill weed

Cream tofu in the blender or mixer, add the avocado, and blend. Then add the lime juice, oil, soy sauce, kelp, and garlic. Add the dill last. This dressing has a limited shelf life (4–5 days) as the avocado will become brown.

Suggestion

- If you are rushed and have some Tofu Mayonnaise (page 37) handy, just add the mashed avocado with lime/lemon squeezed over and a dash of dill.

Preparation time: 8–10 minutes

SPIRAL DRESSING

½ cup sesame oil or safflower or sun-
    flower oil
2 cloves garlic
¼ onion (chunked to blend easily)
3 tablespoons miso (mugi or brown rice)
¼ cup apple cider vinegar
2 tablespoons honey (optional)
½ teaspoon kelp
Dash toasted sesame oil
¼ cup water, approximate, depending on
    preferred consistency
2 tablespoons lecithin syrup or granules

Pour the oil into a blender, add the garlic and onion, and whirl until pulverized. Next add the miso, vinegar, honey, if desired, kelp, toasted sesame oil, and water. Blend in the lecithin last. The lecithin will make the dressing more creamy; it will also make the dressing set when it is chilled.

Suggestions

- I find many miso/vinegar/oil combinations can be used, but the stronger flavors (red/mugi/brown rice misos) tend to combine best with the heavier oils. With hatcho miso or unrefined peanut or sesame oils, use a bit less. Also apple cider vinegar tends to dominate as a flavor, so it holds its own with these more savory misos.
- For a lighter flavor, use sunflower oil or the clear refined oils and rice wine vinegar or lemon or lime juice with white, yellow, or natto miso—don't hesitate to experiment with the proportions suggested above.
- Some miso brands (as a rule, the Japanese ones) are saltier than others. The young pasteurized misos are generally less salty than the venerable, chunky well-aged ones. Many combinations are possible, all with subtly different characters. No wonder the Japanese savor their miso as wine tasters do different vintages.

Preparation time: 10 minutes

Shabu-Shabu

¼ cup sesame (or other) oil
1 clove garlic
1 chunk ginger
¼ cup rice wine vinegar
2 tablespoons lime or lemon juice
2 teaspoons toasted sesame oil
2 tablespoons sesame seeds
2 tablespoons honey
½ teaspoon kelp
¼ cup soy sauce

Pour the oil into the blender, add the garlic and ginger, and blend until smooth. Transfer to a jar with a tight-fitting lid and add the remaining ingredients. Shake until thoroughly blended.

This makes a lovely dressing for a simple green salad of lettuce, sprouts, endive, and green onions.

Suggestion

- For a rich flavored soy sauce, take 3 or 4 garlic bulbs, separate the cloves, peel them, and soak in tamari. Leave them in the tamari indefinitely. If your throat is bothering you or you feel a little under the weather, try eating one of the cloves.

Preparation time: 5–7 minutes

Umeboshi Dressing

⅓–½ cup light oil
1 clove garlic
¼ cup rice wine vinegar
2–3 umeboshi plums, pitted
Dash kelp
1 teaspoon dill weed
1 teaspoon liquid lecithin

Put the oil and garlic in the blender and whiz until the garlic is emulsified. Add the remaining ingredients. Whiz again. This will keep for 2 months in the refrigerator.

Preparation time: 5 minutes

Yeast Onion Dressing

Try this only if you like the taste of nutritional yeast!

¼ cup oil
¼ onion
1 clove garlic
⅛ cup apple cider vinegar
½ teaspoon kelp
2 tablespoons light miso (natto is good)

3 tablespoons nutritional yeast
1 teaspoon lecithin

Put the oil in the blender, add the onion and garlic, and emulsify. Then add the remaining ingredients and blend thoroughly.

Preparation time: 6 minutes

Miso Dressing Does the Hula

½ cup peanut or sesame oil
1 clove garlic
¼ sweet onion
Thumbnail-size chunk ginger, peeled and
    diced
⅛ cup lime or lemon juice
⅛ cup rice wine vinegar
3 tablespoons natto miso
⅛ cup water, approximately, depending on
    desired consistency
½ small papaya, seeds and skin removed
1 tablespoon lecithin
Dash toasted sesame oil
¼ teaspoon kelp
2 tablespoons sesame seeds

Pour the oil in the blender, add the garlic, onion, and ginger, and blend until pulverized. Then add the lime juice, vinegar, natto, water, papaya, lecithin, sesame oil, kelp, and sesame seeds, and whiz away, blending thoroughly. The papaya in this dressing helps it keep; it will last about 2 weeks in the fridge.

Suggestion

• If you're adventurous and you'd like a mild peppery taste, throw in a spoonful or two of the papaya seeds and blend. We love it this way.

Preparation time: 12 minutes

Miso Tahini Gravy

3–4 cloves garlic, pressed or minced
Thumbnail-size chunk of ginger, peeled
   and grated
1 tablespoon oil
⅓ cup tahini
1–2 minced umeboshi plums (optional)
½ teaspoon kelp
Dash toasted sesame oil
¼ cup miso
¼–½ cup water

In a saucepan over low heat, sauté the garlic and ginger in the oil until softened. Stir in the tahini. Add the plums, if desired, and kelp with the sesame oil. Turn off the heat. By now the saucepan should be quite hot. Mix the miso and water. Add it to the oil-tahini-plum mixture. Heat slightly if necessary but *never boil miso* (it kills the good beasties!).

Suggestion

- This sauce blends well with most tofu entrées and is also good over steamed vegetables and grains.

Preparation time: 10–12 minutes

YEAST GRAVY

3 tablespoons wheat germ or whole wheat,
    flour
½ onion, minced
2 cloves garlic
¼ cup oil or tahini or butter
3 tablespoons nutritional yeast
1 teaspoon kelp
¾ cup water
2 tablespoons soy sauce
Black pepper (optional)

Brown the wheat germ or whole wheat flour by dry-roasting in a skillet. Remove it. In the same skillet sauté the onion and garlic in the oil, then stir in the yeast and toasted wheat germ or flour. Slowly add the water and stir constantly. Season with soy sauce last and add pepper if you like. This and the following variation make good toppings for most tofu entrées.

Variation

Shitake Gravy. Use the same ingredients as above, but omit the yeast. Start by soaking 4 or 5 dried mushrooms in the water. When the mushrooms are soft (in about an hour), drain them and save the liquid. Slice the mushrooms into slivers. Use the soaking water to make the gravy. Simmer a bit. Add the soy sauce. This is especially good over brown rice and crisp cooked broccoli.

Preparation time: 10–12 minutes

Gomazio (Toasted Seed Seasoning)

A bowl of brown rice or miso/tofu soup really perks up with this savory topping, and need I add that the oils of the seeds help to complete the protein and amino acid combinations? This recipe is 70 percent technique.

½ **cup sesame seeds, or combination of**
    pumpkin seeds, sunflower seeds, poppy
    seeds, pine nuts
2 **tablespoons soy sauce**
1 **tablespoon kelp**
1 **tablespoon granulated garlic**

Toast seeds in a dry skillet until they're brown and roasted smelling. Add the soy sauce at the last minute, and stir quickly for an even coating. Remove the seeds from the pan as soon as the liquid evaporates (30–60 seconds) and allow them to cool.

If you use a suribachi, grind the seeds until you get a rough textured meal. If you use a food processor, just give the seeds a few quick pulses until most of the seeds are crushed. But don't keep going for a uniform consistency, or you'll end up with paste. Add the kelp and garlic. Store this in an airtight container and try it on everything!

Suggestion

• You might look into purchasing a suribachi (ceramic ribbed bowl with wooden pestle) for crushing your seeds. It's quite beautiful, has many functions, and is usually inexpensive.

Preparation time: 8 minutes in the food processor; 15–20 minutes in the suribachi

Madame Pele's Superlative Salsa

Here's one for the food processor freaks. All ingredients are optional except for the chilies, tomatoes, and onions.

5 large tomatoes or 1 can (28 ounces)
    whole tomatoes and juice
2 medium-size sweet onions
4 fresh chilies or 1/4 cup canned chilies,
    fire roasted
7 green onions
3 garlic cloves
1 small zucchini
1 cucumber (peeled only if waxed)
1 or 2 dried cayenne peppers (small candlestick variety)
1 teaspoon kelp
2 tablespoons soy sauce
2 tablespoons olive oil
½ teaspoon each crushed dried oregano
    and thyme
⅛ cup cilantro
2 vinegar-pickled picante jalapeños (adjust
    these for heat)
⅓–½ cup finely chopped inner celery
    stalks and leaves
2 tablespoons lemon juice *or* mild vinegar

The truly dedicated could hand chop everything. However, the processor freaks will probably dice, chop, and mince everything. You may press the garlic but I would throw it in the processor too. Fresh salsa is best when chunky, so don't emulsify.

Suggestion

- Refrigerate and you'll find it improves on the second day, is great on the third, and becomes a bubbly, fermented volcano in a week or so. Bear this in mind and don't put it in the back of the fridge and forget about it!

Preparation time: 10 minutes in the food processor; 20–22 minutes hand chopping

COMFREY PESTO

Try this alongside the seaweed lasagne.

3 or 4 young comfrey leaves
1 onion
4 cloves garlic
Bouquet of fresh basil, oregano, thyme,
    parsley, inner celery leaves (alone or
    together)
¼ cup green virgin olive oil

1 teaspoon kelp
Parmesan cheese, freshly grated (added or
    on the side)
⅓–½ cup walnuts or pine nuts

Put all ingredients in the processor and whiz.
The fresh greens should provide enough liquid to make a paste.

Preparation time: 10 minutes

MISO SOUP

Most everybody has a favorite miso soup. We developed a species for high-altitude winters in the Rocky Mountains that made it to the table about 20 minutes after we hit the front door. Generally I steer away from frying foods if possible but, for this one, anything goes.

1 carrot
1 stalk broccoli
1 onion
3 cloves garlic
Handful pea pods
½ cup fresh mushrooms (or shitake if you have time to let them soak)
2 tablespoons butter, sesame oil, or olive oil
1 pound tofu, drained, cubed
½ cup dulse, soaked 10 minutes
1 package soba noodles (buckwheat)
¼ cup hatcho miso
Bit of ginger if desired, chunked and peeled
Gomazio (page 48)

Adzuki beans, cooked in advance

Grab all the veggies in the fridge, quick wash and chop, then stir-fry. After the veggies fry in a saucepan, add the tofu, pour water over to cover, and put a lid on the pan for ten minutes. Meanwhile soak the dulse, and pour off the water when done.

Add the soba to the soup. When they are soft, throw in the dulse. Ladle some broth into a cup. Cream the miso into the broth, add it to the pot, and remove from the heat.

A steaming bowl with gomazio sprinkled on top is very close to heaven on the top of the Rockies or anywhere else.

Suggestion

- Try a combination of Swiss chard, spinach, parsnips, and pumpkin instead of the veggies given above.

Preparation time: 20 minutes

Tofu Stands Alone

Here are four ways to prepare your tofu steak (see page 16 for directions on how to prepare tofu steaks) as a speedy entree that will delight initiates to soy products. Please use only peanut oil or olive oil for frying.

Seedy Tofu

Oil
4 tofu cutlets
2 tablespoons sesame seeds
2 tablespoons pumpkin seeds
2 tablespoons sunflower seeds
½ teaspoon Italian herbs
Kelp and garlic granules (to taste)
1 teaspoon soy sauce

In a minimum of oil, fry the cutlets on one side and flip, adding seeds and spices as the second side begins to cook. Add the soy sauce at the last minute. Some like the steaks very brown. For a crispy texture use high heat, but add the seeds only at the end. Others like a softer texture; in this case, use a lower heat.

Preparation time: 12 minutes

Tofu Teriyaki

Prepare Teriyaki Marinade (page 31). Soak four or six cutlets for 2 hours or overnight in the fridge. They will keep in the fridge for 5 days to a week. Drain them. Fry, barbecue, or broil the cutlets and see the eyebrows go up.

Frying time: 6 minutes

Grilled Tofu

This is best for sandwiches and entrées, as it has little water and is not oily. Put a tofu steak on a broiler pan and broil until crispy and brown. Flip and brown slightly, then top with miso paste and a dash of toasted sesame oil and broil until crisp. Miso paste is made by mixing miso with a little water.

Preparation time: 8 minutes

"Chicken" Tofu

My daughter, Loring, came up with this one when she was ten, and what's more, she can prepare it exquisitely by herself.

10 tofu steaks
1/4 cup soy sauce
Kelp and garlic granules
Powdered ginger
Nutritional yeast

Soak the steaks in the soy sauce, then sprinkle with the kelp, garlic, and ginger to your taste. Pour off the excess liquid and flour the outside of the steaks with the yeast.

Fry the steaks quickly but don't burn the yeast. Now it tastes a lot like those feathered friends some of us don't want to eat.

Preparation time: 10 minutes

Tofu Vegetable Scramble

My bacon-and-eggs little brother perfected this one!
It's good for breakfast, lunch, or dinner.

1 onion, diced
2 garlic cloves, pressed
½ green pepper, diced
1 tablespoon oil
5 or 6 large mushrooms, sliced
1 cup drained tofu, crumbled
1 zucchini, shredded (optional)

Now, any of the following:
⅓ cup white tiger sauce *or* oriental mushroom sauce *or* steak sauce

Or make your own:
2 tablespoons catsup
½ teaspoon honey
¼ teaspoon Worcestershire sauce
½ teaspoon soy sauce
½ teaspoon kelp
¼ teaspoon ground cumin powder

¼ teaspoon cayenne pepper
Dash apple cider vinegar

Sauté the onion, garlic, and green pepper in the oil. Add the mushrooms and tofu. Grate the zucchini over the top; add the sauce. Simmer until everything is soft (about 4 minutes). Turn off the heat. If you like, melt grated cheddar or Swiss on the top or add fresh ground pepper or a bit of Gomazio (page 48). Top with a handful of alfalfa sprouts and you have a mouthful.

We serve this with steamed, buttered tortillas.

Suggestion

- Instead of the sautéed vegetables, last night's steamed veggie leftovers will do nicely—broccoli, green beans, spinach, Swiss chard, corn, tomatoes.

Preparation time: 12–15 minutes

CREAMED TOFU CURRY

One summer night we knocked ourselves out with this one. We had no idea creaming the curry with tofu would work so well.

¼ cup oil or butter
½ green apple, chopped
1 handful dried currants
4 cloves garlic, minced
2 bay leaves
3 tablespoons curry powder *or* your
    favorite mix—ground cumin, ground
    coriander, ground cardamom, ground
    cinnamon, ground cloves, turmeric
½ cup fresh green peas
½ cup carrot rounds
½ cup potato cubes
2 tablespoons soy sauce
3 cups water
½ cup fresh, cooked deveined shrimp
    (optional)
1 ¼ pounds tofu

In a heavy saucepan with a lid, heat the oil and sauté the next three ingredients in it, then add the spices, veggies, soy sauce, and water. Bring to a boil, lower the heat, and simmer until the veggies are soft. If you're using shrimp add them the last 3 or 4 minutes of the veggie boil time. Take some of the broth from the soup and cream the tofu in the blender until smooth. Add this mixture to the pan and warm thoroughly. Serve over hot, brown rice with the usual condiments: yogurt, coconut, green onion, mango, peanuts, and chutneys. These last few items are a distinct transgression of food-combining rules but, hey, we're not being too rigid, remember?

Preparation time: 40 minutes

Not-So Latin Lasagne

Allow the tomato sauce to simmer for at least 2 hours.

12 or 14 long green lasagne noodles
3 strips of wakame seaweed (about)

Tomato Sauce

1 large onion
2 cloves garlic
3–4 inner stalks celery
2 tablespoons olive oil
2 teaspoons dried oregano
1 teaspoon dried thyme
1 can (28 ounces) whole tomatoes, well
    drained
1 can (6 ounces) tomato paste
½ teaspoon ground clove
1 tablespoon honey
1 teaspoon soy sauce
Water

Filling

Drained crumbled tofu (1 ½–2 blocks, 1 ½
    pounds)
¼ cup sunflower seeds
1 cup grated zucchini or crookneck squash
20–40 black olives sliced (optional)
1 cup sliced fresh mushrooms

Topping

11–12 ounces mozzarella, sliced
⅓ cup freshly grated Parmesan

Boil the lasagne until barely softened, about 6 minutes; drain and cool. Soak the seaweed for about 20 minutes; drain and cut the fibrous central stem from the seaweed. Cut it into lengths that equal the noodles.

To prepare the sauce, sauté the onion, garlic, and celery in the olive oil. Crush the herbs over the veggies, then add the tomatoes, paste, cloves, honey, soy sauce, and water to thin. Simmer for 2 or 3 hours if possible.

Mash the filling ingredients together and add an egg if necessary for cohesiveness.

In an oblong baking dish, layer the noodles, filling, seaweed, sauce, and Parmesan twice and top with slices of mozzarella. Bake at 350° F. (180° C.) for about 45 minutes.

If possible, give the lasagne a chance to cool and pull itself together for 15 minutes before serving. This makes dinner for 4–6 people, 8 with modest appetites.

Preparation time: 35 minutes plus 45 minutes to bake lasagne

Spaghetti with Soya Meatballs

A quick version of this if you don't have the time to make these meatballs is to quick-fry a block of crumbled tofu and toss it in the marinara sauce for a protein additive.

3 cups boiled soybeans, drained
½ cup sesame seeds
2 onions, chopped
¼ cup oil
¼ cup soy sauce
1 tablespoon each kelp and garlic granules

You must allow a long preparation time because it takes 2 or 3 hours to cook the beans. They should mash easily between the fingers. But this freezes well, so you can double the amount to make best use of your preparation time. Always remember to soak the beans 8 hours before cooking and to toss out initial soaking water.

Mash the soybeans to a paste, or put them in a processor. Dry roast the sesame seeds and add them to the mashed beans. Sauté the onions in the oil, and add the soy sauce. In the last 2 or 3 minutes add the kelp and garlic granules, and stir all ingredients together for a standard use-it-anywhere soybean burger, or for meatballs.

Marinara Sauce

1 large can (28 ounces) whole tomatoes
    with juice, mashed
1 can (6 ounces) tomato paste
2 cups water to thin
1 onion
1 inner stalk celery
1 thin slice zucchini
4 cloves garlic
1 tablespoon honey
1 tablespoon soy sauce
½ teaspoon each dried oregano, dried
    thyme, and dried rosemary
½ teaspoon ground cloves
1 bay leaf
⅓ cup olive oil
Chopped parsley (optional)
Ground sage (optional)
Ground cumin (optional)
½ cup wheat germ
Parmesan cheese

Mix the sauce ingredients together in a pot, bring to a boil, cover, and simmer 40 minutes or for hours. While the sauce is simmering, use the prepared soy meat to form meatballs. Add some chopped parsley and sage and ground cumin if you like. Roll the balls in wheat germ and brown them in olive oil. If they seem to be breaking apart in the frying process, add a little brown rice flour or an egg, or both. Set meatballs aside.

Cook about 8 ounces sesame, spinach, or whole wheat noodles. Add the meatballs to the sauce and serve with the cooked noodles and fresh Parmesan.

Preparation time: 20 minutes; 2 hours to boil beans; 40 minutes or several hours

Tofu Pizza

My feeling is, that if you're going to eat pizza, make your own crust, pile on the goodies, and smother it in cheese. But shortcuts can be taken: try French bread broiled with garlic-olive oil spread over for a base, or crisped pita bread for the cracker-type crusts.

Crust

1 cake active yeast or 1 tablespoon dry yeast
⅓ to ½ cup warm water
1 teaspoon malt syrup, honey, or molasses
2 cups whole wheat bread flour (or barley or oat flour)
¼ cup olive oil, plus extra for the pans
¼ cup cornmeal flour

Toppings

Thin-sliced purple or red onion rings
Thin-sliced tomatoes
Thin-sliced green peppers
Mushrooms (sautéed first for fuller flavor)
Anchovies or umeboshi strips
Browned round bits of soysage
Turkey sausage (for the die-hard carnivore)
Black or green olives
Grated carrot
Artichoke hearts
Marinara Sauce (page 58)
Mozzarella, cheddar, Jarlsberg cheese
Layer of Parmesan

To prepare the crust, dissolve the yeast in the water with the sweetening and place in a warm spot. When it bubbles to the top, mix it in a bowl with the flour, stir well, and add the oil. You can put in a dash of soy sauce if you like some salt in your crust. Cover and let rise for 30–45 minutes. The dough should hopefully be elastic and manageable (flour or oil your hands). Now oil the pizza pans, dust with the cornmeal, and spread the dough to the edges. Put aside to rise again while you set to chopping and slicing your favorite ingredients, choosing from the list given.

Now, using about 1 cup per pizza of the marinara sauce, spread it over the now-risen doughs. If you are short of time, a thin layer of tomato pace will suffice. Strew or place the toppings, according to your mood. Top generously with the cheese of your choice and a layer of Parmesan. Bake at 400° F. (200° C.) for 30 to 40 minutes to 1 hour. Makes 2 pizzas.

Preparation time: 15 minutes; 1 hour to let the crust rise; 35 minutes to cook the pizza

TOFU VEGGIE PIE

Now, you will have to understand that pastry shells for pie and I have never gotten along. So either choose your favorite whole wheat recipe and add a few teaspoons of poppy seeds or try the recipe below. It worked last time I used it.

3 tablespoons butter
3 ½–4 cups chopped veggies: carrots, parsnips, potatoes, green peas, pea pods, pumpkin, lima beans, cut green beans, broccoli and cauliflower chunks and florets, Swiss chard, mushrooms, celery, spinach, onions, green onions, garlic
⅓ cup water
2 tablespoons tahini
2 tablespoons miso
2 tablespoons flour (brown rice flour works well)
½ teaspoon each dried thyme and dried marjoram, *or* curry spices

Pie Crust

2 cups whole wheat flour
½ cup brown rice flour
⅔ cup butter or oil
⅓–½ cup cold water
1 teaspoon sea salt
3 teaspoons poppy seeds

Heat the butter in a large skillet and sauté the vegetables for about 10 minutes.

Mix the water with the tahini, miso, and seasonings. Then sprinkle the flour over it, mix well, and pour it into a pan. Cook until thickened and smooth. Then add to the large skillet.

Stir the gravy until it coats the vegetables. Pour everything into the prepared pie shell. Cover with top crust. Bake at 375° F. (180° C.) for 45–50 minutes. Turn down the heat at the end if the crust gets too brown. Cool and let the pie set for 15–20 minutes. Serve with yogurt or sour cream.

Preparation time: 1 1/2 hours

Tofu Olé Enchiladas

Enchilada Sauce

1 can (6 ounces) tomato paste
1 cup water
Dash cayenne, chili powder, kelp, soy sauce
½ cup sour cream (optional)

½ pound tofu drained and crumbled
1 cup grated sharp cheddar, divided
½ cup grated Monterey jack
¼ cup chopped black olives
2 medium onions, chopped
12 corn tortillas

Combine the Enchilada Sauce ingredients and warm it up (or buy a 6–8 ounce can of enchilada sauce).

In a bowl, stir together the tofu, ½ cup cheddar, Monterey jack, olives, and onions. Dip the tortillas in the sauce one at a time, removing after a minute or two. It should be coated with sauce, malleable, but not crumbling apart. Lay each one out flat in an oblong casserole, put a handful of stuffing in the center, and roll into a tube. Line them up to fill the casserole. Take the remaining sauce and pour over the top. You can thin it with water to spread it further or add the sour cream if you like it rich. Sprinkle the rest of the cheddar over the top, bake at 350° F. for 30 minutes. Remove the pan from the oven and give the enchiladas 10 minutes to cool and collect themselves before serving.

Preparation time: 1 hour 10 minutes

Tofu Samosa

Jackets

1 ½ cups whole wheat flour
2 tablespoons oil
5 tablespoons water
¼ teaspoon soy sauce
Poppy seeds (optional)

Filling

1 onion, chopped
1 cup crumbled tofu
½ cup grated carrot
⅓ cup chopped steamed cauliflower
½ cup cubed, cooked potatoes
1 teaspoon cumin seed
1 teaspoon curry
1 teaspoon mustard seed
½ teaspoon garlic granules
Soy sauce (to taste)

To prepare the jackets, sift the flour. Add the oil and mix until evenly distributed. Mix the water and soy sauce together and dribble over the dough. Work into a cohesive mass. Add the seeds, if desired. Separate into ping pong-size balls and roll them out on a floured board into 8-inch-diameter circles.

Prepare the filling by mixing the first five ingredients in a bowl. Sprinkle the seasonings and soy sauce over the top. Stir, blending uniformly.

Fill the rolled-out jackets with the tofu mixture, lap one-half over, and seal the edges with water. Scallop with your thumb and forefinger.

Bake at 375° to 400° F. for 30 minutes on an oiled oven tray until the pastry browns around the edges. Eat hot or cold with mustard.

Preparation time: 1 hour 10 minutes

SPANAKOPETA PARCELS

1 packet of whole wheat filo sheets (if
   available)
½ cup melted butter or ¼ cup butter and
   ¼ cup olive oil
Large bunch spinach
½ cup feta
½ cup drained tofu, crumbled
1 onion, chopped
1 egg
Lots of pressed garlic

Read the filo directions carefully and unwrap
one sheet. Fold it square. Butter it with a
brush. Layer it with another and butter. Layer
one more sheet. Prepare 4 or 5 squares.

Clean the spinach and chop it. Drain it
well. Soak the feta to remove excess salt, crumble,
and drain. In a bowl, mix together the
spinach, feta, tofu, and onion with the egg and
pressed garlic. Stir until evenly blended. Cover
one triangular half of the prepared filo with a
layer of the spinach mix. Fold the other half
triangle over the top of the filling and moisten
slightly to seal. Repeat with the remaining
squares. Bake at 400° F. for 20–30 minutes.
The filo paper will be crispy and browned on
the edges. These are great hot or cold.

Preparation time: 1 hour

Tofu Quiche

Use the same crust as in Tofu Veggie Pie (page 62), but substitute sesame seeds for poppy seeds and halve the recipe for bottom crust only.

2 tablespoons butter
½ cup thin-sliced mushrooms
1 cup tofu, in pieces
2 eggs
½ cup shredded Swiss cheese
4 medium green onions, chopped, with
    some tops included
2 tablespoons soy sauce
1 teaspoon each kelp and garlic granules
1 teaspoon dried thyme
1 teaspoon dried marjoram
¼ cup pumpkin seeds
¼ cup sunflower seeds
⅓ cup fresh grated Parmesan

Heat the butter in a small skillet, add the mushrooms, and sauté until soft. Cool.

Crumble the tofu in a bowl, beat in the eggs, and cream with an electric mixer until smooth. Add the cheese and onions; stir with a spoon. Add the soy sauce and seasonings. Stir in the cooled mushrooms and set aside.

In a blender, grind the pumpkin and sunflower seeds to a meal, add the cheese, and whiz again. Pour the tofu mixture into the prepared pie shell, sprinkle the seed and cheese mixture on top, and bake at 350° to 375° F. for 40 minutes or until done in the center. Cool slightly and slice into wedges.

Preparation time: 1 hour 20 minutes

SEED CRUST SOUFFLÉ

Crust

¼ cup pumpkin seeds
¼ cup sunflower seeds
⅓ cup Parmesan
1 teaspoon kelp
1 tablespoon butter

Soufflé

3 tablespoons butter
2–3 tablespoons whole wheat flour, arrowroot, or brown rice flour
1 cup milk, cream, or thick soy milk
6 eggs, separated
1 ½ cups grated emmenthaler or Gruyère cheese
4–6 onions, finely chopped
2 teaspoons fresh basil
1 teaspoon dried thyme

Preheat the oven to 425° F.

Prepare the crust by grinding the seeds in a blender; add the Parmesan and blend again. Slather the butter on the inside of a soufflé dish, dust with the seed mix, and set aside.

To make the soufflé, melt the butter and remove from the heat. Stir in the flour until evenly blended, in the same manner as making a white sauce. Gradually add a bit of milk or cream, stirring until all can be added without lumps. Return to the heat and stir faithfully until thickened. Add 4 egg yolks, 1 at a time, stirring unflaggingly. By now a fairly thick custard should set up. (Save the other 2 egg yolks for another creation.) Stir in about half the cheese until it's melted and remove from the heat. Beat all 6 egg whites until fluffy and peaked but not dry. Set aside.

Add the onions and herbs with the remaining cheese to the cheese custard. Fold in the egg whites until they are fairly evenly distributed.

Pour gently into the prepared dish and cook at 425° F. for 30–40 minutes or until browned on top and well risen. Serve without delay if you want to hear all those indrawn breaths of anticipation.

Preparation time: 1 hour 10 minutes

Soy Sprout Fu Yung with Natto Sauce

5 eggs
1 teaspoon kelp
1 garlic clove, crushed
2 tablespoons soy sauce
2–2 ½ cups soy sprouts
8 green onions, sliced with green tops
  included
1 cup thinly sliced celery
1 cup thinly sliced mushrooms
½ cup small deveined shrimp (optional)
⅓–½ cup sliced bamboo shoots and/or
  water chestnuts (optional)
Peanut oil

To make the fu yung, beat the eggs with the seasonings and soy sauce. Add the veggies and shrimp, if desired, coating evenly. Spoon into a large skillet with preheated oil. Brown quickly on both sides and drain on paper towels.

Natto Sauce

3 tablespoons tahini
¾ cup water, divided
2 tablespoons arrowroot, cornstarch, or
  kudzu
1 clove garlic, crushed
Dab of honey
2 tablespoons rice wine vinegar (if you like
  sweet/sour) *or* lemon or pineapple juice
½ cup natto miso

To prepare the sauce, cream the tahini and ¼ cup water slowly until pasty in a saucepan over medium-low heat until the mixture forms a paste. Then, in a jar with lid, shake the remaining ½ cup water with the arrowroot and add to the pan. Cook, stirring, until it is thickened. Add the garlic, honey, and vinegar. Mix some sauce and the natto in a bowl until you get a smooth paste, then return all to the pan. Bring up to barely steaming and shut off the heat. Do not boil. Spoon over the fu yung just before serving.

Preparation time: 25 minutes

CORN PORRIDGE WITH TOFU CUBES

A savory breakfast production, this dish is good for those who prefer a warm morning meal. Spread any leftovers in a flat glass casserole to cool. They will solidify and can be cut into squares and refried for an evening snack.

2 cups water
2–3 cloves garlic, chopped
1 onion, chopped
2 sprigs parsley, chopped
1 zucchini, sliced thin
½ polenta or cornmeal
½ teaspoon dried thyme
1 teaspoon dried oregano
1 tomato, chopped
1 handful dulse or karengo

1 cup tofu cubes (presoaked in soy sauce and drained)
4 ounces cheddar, jack, or Swiss cheese, in chunks (optional)
Sprinkle soy sauce (to taste)
1 teaspoon kelp

Bring the water to a boil with the garlic, onion, parsley, and zucchini. When they are soft (about 6 minutes), drizzle in the polenta, stirring as you go. Let it gently boil, stirring occasionally, adding the herbs, tomato, and dulse. It will thicken quickly. Finally, stir in the tofu cubes. If cheese cubes are desired, add them last. Serve with a bit of soy sauce and a sprinkle of kelp.

Preparation time: 18 minutes

CREAM OF TOFU POTATO LEEK SOUP

2 ½ cups cubed potatoes
1 cup sliced leeks, well washed
1 cup celery, all inner leaves and heart
  included
1 onion, chopped
4 cups water
3 cloves garlic, chopped
3 sprigs parsley, chopped
1 teaspoon dried thyme
½ teaspoon dried rosemary
2 tablespoons butter (optional)
½ block (12 ounces) silken tofu
2 tablespoons light miso

Boil the vegetables in the water with the garlic, parsley, and seasonings for 40 minutes. Add the butter. Cream the tofu in a blender, adding some of the vegetable stock if necessary, until smooth. Add it to the soup. Using more stock, cream the miso and use it to season the soup to your taste. This is great topped with Gomazio (page 48).

Preparation time: 12 minutes; 40 minutes to cook the soup

TEMPEH STICKS

These make a great hors d'oeuvre or protein dish for a light veggie meal. Some find they taste like mushrooms, or even frogs' legs.

8-inch-square tempeh, sliced in sticks like French fries
Peanut oil

Deep-fry the tempeh until crispy brown in the oil and drain. Or pan-fry thinnish fingers, browning them thoroughly on both sides. Prepare one of the following dips and serve.

Cocktail Tomato Dip

¾ cup catsup
Dash soy sauce
Dash Worcestershire sauce
Juice of ½ lemon or lime
1 teaspoon honey
Kelp and garlic granules

Soy Sauce Dip

¼ cup soy sauce
Dash toasted sesame oil
Juice of ½ lemon
Kelp and garlic granules

Preparation time: 20 minutes

Lentil Dosa

1 cup dry lentils
1 carrot, sliced or shredded
1 onion, chopped
2 garlic cloves, diced
2 ¾ cups water, divided
¼ cup miso
1 teaspoon curry powder
2 tablespoons tahini
6–8 tortillas, or chapatis

Garnish

Grated cheese
Alfalfa sprouts
Diced tomatoes
Sour cream

Boil the lentils, carrot, onion, and garlic in 2 ½ cups water until the lentils are soft. Set aside and allow to cool. The mixture should hang together without being soupy.

Pour the remaining water into a cup, blend in the miso, curry, and tahini, and stir into the lentils. Keep this mixture warm.

Steam the tortillas or warm them in the oven. Put the lentil mixture in the center of each tortilla, add whatever garnishes you want, and wrap the tortilla. Now it can be picked up and eaten as is. If the lentils are too soupy, then resort to a plate and fork for neater eating.

Preparation time: 55 minutes

LIMA BEANS TAHINI

No, this is not a Polynesian nightclub headliner! But it is enough to make dyed-in-the-wool lima bean haters give them a try.

1 pound dry lima beans
¼ cup tahini
1 onion, chopped
2 cloves garlic, minced
1 tablespoon kelp
1 tablespoon honey
2 teaspoons ground or 1 teaspoon whole cumin seed
½ teaspoon dill seed
2 tablespoons lemon juice
2 big tablespoons miso (natto is great, or brown rice miso)

Soak the beans overnight. Drain off the soaking water. In a saucepan, add just enough fresh water to cover the beans. Bring to a boil, cover the pan, and simmer until almost soft, about 1 ½ hours.

Add the remaining ingredients, except the lemon juice and miso. Finish simmering the beans until they fall apart in your mouth. Blend the lemon juice and miso and stir in.

Remove from the heat. The less water there remains in the broth, the more gravy-like the result.

Preparation time: 8 minutes; 1 1/2 hours to cook the beans

DINNER YAMS

This preparation goes for any yam or sweet potato.

1 yam
Soy sauce
Kelp and garlic granules
Mushrooms, sliced
Green onion, sliced
Dabs of grain mustard
Cheese, Swiss, Gruyère, or edam, sliced

Wash, dry, and coat the yam in olive oil or toasted sesame oil. Place on the oven rack and bake at 350° F. for 40–45 minutes, or until soft. Remove it from the oven, and split it open. Sprinkle with the soy sauce and seasonings. Then add a layer of mushrooms, onion, and mustard, and top with a slice of cheese.

Return the yam to the oven when assembled and bake until the cheese is melted and bubbly. This is nice served with a handful of alfalfa spouts.

Preparation time: 45 minutes

SOY MILK SMOOTHIE

Here comes a wonderful protein breakfast.

1 cup unsweetened or vanilla soy milk
1 cup chilled fruit pieces, choose from
 bananas, papayas, mangoes, cranber-
 ries, pineapple, nectarines, peaches, any
 berries
½ cup freshly squeezed orange, lemon, or
 lime juice
⅓ cup soy or dairy yogurt
1 teaspoon liquid (or granulated) lecithin
 (optional)
2 tablespoons protein powder (optional)

Ice cubes (optional)
2 tablespoons coconut (if you like crunchy
 texture)
2 tablespoons bee pollen

Blend the soy milk, fruit, juice (for variety, try passionfruit juice), yogurt, and lecithin, if desired. Add the protein powder if you have a favorite. Add ice cubes, if desired, and blend again. Pour into a glass and top with coconut and pollen.

Preparation time: 6 minutes

SLIPPERY ELM SMOOTHIE

1 tablespoon slippery elm powder
3 tablespoons cold water
2 cups hot water
1 ½ tablespoons honey
Juice of ½ orange
Juice of ½ lemon
¼ teaspoon freshly ground nutmeg
¼ teaspoon ground cinnamon

Soak the slippery elm powder in the cold water until a smooth blob results. Whiz it in a blender with the hot water until frothy. Add the honey, fruit juice, and spices. Blend again and serve in mugs. This soothing drink is a great nightcap for a grumbly stomach.

Preparation time: 5 minutes

MISSING EGG NOG

2 tablespoons slippery elm powder *or* sea
    farine
¼ cup cold water
3 cups soy milk
2 bananas (fairly firm and prefrozen if you
    like a thick texture)
¼ cup honey or maple syrup
1 teaspoon ground cinnamon
½ teaspoon ground cardamom
1 tablespoon vanilla extract
¼ teaspoon freshly grated nutmeg

Soak the slippery elm powder in the water. It should form a mucilaginous blob when fully soaked. Put it in a blender with the soy milk and whirl. Add the bananas, honey, and spices, and blend again. Add the vanilla last. Pour into chilled glasses and grind a dash of nutmeg on top.

Preparation time: 10 minutes

Carob Banana Shake

⅓ cup sea farine *or* 2 tablespoons slippery elm
¼ cup cold water
2 cups soy milk
3 tablespoons honey or molasses or maple syrup
1 teaspoon vanilla extract
¼ cup toasted carob powder
1 or 2 ripe bananas (prechilled)
Grated coconut, for garnish
Ice

Soak the sea farine or slippery elm in the water. Blend it when soft with the soy milk, sweetener, and vanilla. Add the carob and whiz; add the bananas and whiz. Pour into chilled glasses topped with coconut sprinkle. If you like it thick, add ice at the last minute.

Preparation time: 6 minutes

BANANA DATE SHAKE WITH ALMONDS

2 ripe bananas
10–12 pitted dates
About 20 raw almonds or cashews
½ teaspoon vanilla extract
2 tablespoons molasses or honey (if you
   like it sweet)
2 cups plain or vanilla soy milk
2 teaspoons flax seeds, soaked overnight
Dash fresh ground nutmeg

Blend all the ingredients in a blender until the nuts and seeds are fairly well ground. Add a few ice cubes to chill and blend again. You can thicken this with 2 teaspoons sea farine or 1 teaspoon agar-agar dissolved in   cup cold water, allowing it to stand for 5 minutes. Alternately, 1 teaspoon of psyllium seed husks prepared in the same way could provide your daily bulk, too. Top with nutmeg.

    Drink before the bananas brown. This is not a keeper.

Preparation time: 8 minutes

Mamma Miso's Cuppa

Make this paste and keep it in a sealed container in the fridge. A batch lasts longer if you omit the onions and add them at the time of preparation. We don't keep it around very long because everybody eats it by the spoonful when they get peckish. Natto miso is sensational here but brown rice, white, or yellow will do.

½ cup miso
½ cup tahini
⅓ cup peanut butter
1 mild onion, diced
4 cloves garlic, minced
½ teaspoon toasted sesame oil
¼ cup sesame seeds (chia seeds too)
1 tablespoon kelp
1 thumb of fresh ginger, minced
Dulse or karengo
Soba noodles

To make the paste, cream together the first five ingredients. Then stir in the oil, seeds, kelp, and ginger.

Soak the seaweed and drain it. Boil some water, throw in some noodles, and cook until tender (4–5 minutes).

Put about 2 tablespoons of miso mix paste in a mug, cream with a little boiled water, and then almost fill the mug. Add the noodles and seaweed, some cubed tofu, and possibly a few green onion slices. Stir, and wow!—a whole meal in one cup in 5 minutes.

Preparation time: 8 minutes to make paste; 4 minutes to boil noodles; 2 minutes to mix soup

Tahini Chew Cookies

½ **cup tahini**

¼ **cup oil**

½ **cup honey or malt syrup** *or* ⅓ **cup raisin butter**

1 cup rolled oats

⅓ **cup walnuts**

⅓ **cup sesame seeds or half/half with sunflower seeds**

¼ **cup chopped dates or sultanas (optional)**

1 teaspoon vanilla extract

Dash salt (optional)

Mix the tahini and oil by stirring slowly. Then add the honey or raisin butter and cream the mix. Stir in the oats, walnuts, sesame seeds, and dates. Add the vanilla last and salt, if desired. The dough will be quite stiff. Place teaspoon-size mounds on an oiled cookie sheet and press flat with a fork in a crisscross pattern. Bake at 325° F. for 12–15 minutes.

Preparation time: 30 minutes

GINGERBREAD CAKE WITH
MOLASSES CREAM CHEESE ICING

Dry Ingredients

1 cup brown rice flour
½ cup whole wheat pastry flour
1 teaspoon baking powder
2 teaspoons ground ginger
½ teaspoon ground cinnamon
½ teaspoon ground cloves
1 teaspoon baking powder

Wet Ingredients

½ cup butter (or ¼ cup butter and ¼ cup oil)
⅓ cup honey
⅓ cup molasses
2 eggs
¼ cup soy milk
2 teaspoons vanilla extract
⅓ chopped cup walnuts

Icing

8 ounces cream cheese, at room temperature
¼ cup molasses
1 teaspoon vanilla extract
1 teaspoon grated lemon rind
¼ cup orange juice or juice of 1 lemon

Sift the dry ingredients.

In a mixing bowl, cream the butter and add the honey and molasses. Beat in the eggs one at a time, stir in the soy milk, and beat well.

Add the flour mixture gradually, beating until smooth. Stir in the vanilla and walnuts. Pour into a buttered 8 x 8-inch cake tin and bake at 375° F. (180° C.) for 30–45 minutes. Cool for 10 minutes. Remove from the pan and cool on a rack.

To make the icing, beat the softened cream cheese until smooth. Add the molasses, vanilla, lemon rind, and orange juice or the juice of a lemon. If necessary, chill the icing a little to aid spreading. Spread it on top of the gingerbread cake.

Preparation time: 20 minutes; 40 minutes to bake cake

DATE-FILLED WHOLE WHEAT BARS

This is a superb snack/dessert, but you need to have at least some kind of dried fruit to make it. I love dates, but dried apricots, peaches, plums, prunes, cherries, even sultanas, can work well.

Crust

⅓ **cup sunflower seeds**
⅓ **cup sesame seeds**
⅓ **cup coconut, desiccated**
¾ **cup rolled oats**
½ **cup brown rice flour**
1 **teaspoon ground cinnamon**
½ **cup chopped walnuts**
⅓ **cup butter**
3 **tablespoons honey**
1 ½ **teaspoons vanilla extract**

Topping

¼ **cup butter**
⅓ **cup honey or malt syrup for a really chewy center**
½ **cup fairly fresh dates, pitted and chopped or mashed**

To prepare the crust, roast the seeds, cool, and in a bowl combine with the other dry ingredients and nuts, mixing thoroughly. Melt the butter with the honey until only just liquefied. Add the vanilla. Pour this over the dry mixture and blend thoroughly. Butter an 8 x 8-inch baking dish and pat or press half of this nut mix into the bottom for a crust.

To make the topping, melt the butter and honey together, and when it's liquid, add the dates and stir to an even consistency. When everything is thoroughly emulsified (about 5 minutes cooking over a low heat), it's ready to spread on the crust. Top with the remaining nut mix and pat down. Bake at 375° F. for 25–30 minutes or until the crust is golden brown. Cool and cut into bars.

Preparation time: 20 minutes; 25 minutes to bake

TOFU CHEESECAKE

Filling

2 cups creamed silken tofu
¼ cup cashew butter
2 tablespoons tahini
½–¾ cup honey
1 egg (optional)
1 ½ teaspoon grated lemon rind
¼ teaspoon grated nutmeg
⅓ cup fresh squeezed orange juice
1 teaspoon ground cinnamon
2 tablespoons lecithin
2 tablespoons vanilla extract

Crust

⅓ cup butter
2 tablespoons honey
20–25 honey graham crackers
¼ cup crushed walnuts

To make the filling, cream the tofu in a blender or with a hand mixer until very smooth. Add the nut/seed butters and cream again. Blend in the honey (a dash of maple syrup wouldn't go astray here, either). If you want to add an egg, beat it in now.

Throw in the lemon rind, nutmeg, orange juice, cinnamon, and lecithin. Beat with a mixer until a smooth, soft texture results. Add vanilla. Set aside.

To prepare the crust, melt the butter in a saucepan, stir in the honey, and blend. Don't boil.

Crush the graham crackers with rolling pin, then add with the nuts to the melted butter. Stir to make an even, crumbly mass. Press into the pie tin or spring-form pan. Pour the tofu filling over the crust and bake at 375° F. (180° C.) for 30–40 minutes, or until the crust is brown and the tofu firms. Chill well. Garnish with orange slices, strawberries, or walnuts. Or try a garnish of borage or violet flowers, or even nasturtiums with a mango glaze.

Preparation time: 20 minutes; 30-40 minutes to bake

TOFU/PUMPKIN CUSTARD PIE

1 pie shell
½–⅓ cup chopped walnuts
1 cup tofu
2 cups puréed cooked pumpkin
1 egg (optional)
½ cup honey
2 tablespoons lecithin
1 ½ teaspoons ground ginger
½ teaspoon grated nutmeg
2 teaspoons ground cinnamon
½ teaspoon ground cloves
½ teaspoon ground coriander
½ teaspoon ground cardamom
1–2 teaspoons vanilla extract

Prepare a pastry shell, adding the chopped walnuts.

Cream the tofu, pumpkin, and egg, if you want, together. Add the honey, lecithin, and spices. Cream thoroughly and add the vanilla last, mixing thoroughly. Pour into the pie shell. If you like a very smooth texture, blend the tofu until creamy, add pumpkin purée and lecithin, and blend again. It will be quite thick so stir in the spices and vanilla and pour into the pie shell.

Bake at 400° F. for 50 minutes to 1 hour, until the center of the custard bounces back when tapped. Lower the temperature to 350° F. if the crust browns too quickly. Gild the lily and try the pie with whipped cream (made from 1 cup chilled cream, 2 tablespoons honey, and 1 1/2 teaspoons vanilla extract) or ice cream.

Preparation time: 1 1/2 hours

Seed Nut Crepes

⅓ cup sesame seeds
⅓ cup sunflower seeds
¼ cup almonds, pecan, walnuts, or
    cashews
¼ cup flaked coconut
¼ cup raisins or sultanas
3 or 4 dates (optional)
2 cups water
1 cup rolled oats
½ cup brown rice flour
⅓ cup whole wheat flour
½ cup wheat germ
3 tablespoons oil or melted butter
1 egg (optional, it helps cohesiveness)
1 teaspoon vanilla extract

Soak the seeds, nuts, coconut, and dried fruit in the water overnight.

Dry grind the oats and mix with the two flours and wheat germ. In the blender grind up the soaked ingredients. Pour them into a bowl, add the shortening, and stir. Now add the dry ingredients and stir. Blend in the egg, if desired, and vanilla and mix thoroughly. Heat a crepe pan or heavy skillet and brush with oil. Drop about 2–3 tablespoons batter in the center of the pan and spread to thin the crepe by tilting the pan to cover the bottom surface. Batter should be cohesive enough to permit turning. Cook until crisp on both sides.

While warm, serve with melted butter, either rolling goodies inside, or serve like pancakes pouring fruit and syrup over the top. Some suggestions for topping are yogurt, whipped cream, fresh fruit with honey, ice cream, maple syrup, Sesame Brittle (page 95) in liquid form.

Preparation time: 25 minutes

Chocolate Fondue

1 cup brandy
1/2 vanilla bean *or* 2 teaspoons vanilla
    extract (optional)
4 ounces unsweetened chocolate
¼–⅓ cup honey
1 cup heavy cream or ¾ cup thick coconut
    cream for dairy free
1 ounce Grand Marnier or Crème de
    Menthe or Kahlua (optional)

Heat the brandy, add the vanilla bean as you heat, but do not boil. If you are using extract, add it last. When the brandy mixture is hot but not boiling, melt the chocolate in, stirring constantly. Add honey to taste. Add the cream gradually, stirring constantly. If desired, add the liqueur of your choice. Keep warm over a small flame or a small alcohol burner.

Here are some choices of stuff to dip in the fondue: frozen ice cream balls, pecan halves, walnut halves, cashews; pieces of sponge or pound cake; chilled fruit bits, frosted in the freezer, such as pineapple, strawberries, blackberries, papaya, mango, raspberries, peaches, orange segments, bananas, pitted cherries. The list is endless!

Preparation time: 15 minutes

TOFU RAISIN RICE PUDDING

1 ½ cups cooked brown rice
½ cup silken tofu, creamed or crumbled
1 egg, beaten (optional)
½ cup raisins or currants
⅓ cup walnuts, almonds, or sunflower
  seeds
1 teaspoon ground cinnamon
1 teaspoon vanilla extract
½ teaspoon each freshly ground nutmeg,
  coriander, and allspice
3 tablespoons butter

¼ cup honey, malt syrup, or molasses
2 tablespoons maple syrup

Mix the first 8 ingredients in a bowl. Melt the butter with the honey or malt syrup and add it to the rice mix. Cook in a glass casserole dish at 350° F. (180° C.) for about 40 minutes. Drizzle the maple syrup over the top.

Preparation time: 1 hour 10 minutes

Polar Bean

Choose your own flavor here.

3 tablespoons slippery elm powder
¼ cup cold water
3–4 cups rich soy milk, divided
½ cup honey or maple syrup
2 teaspoons vanilla extract
Dash sea salt

Flavor of your choice:
1. **1 cup raspberries, (fresh chilled), with the juice of ½ lemon squeezed over**
2. **½–⅓ cup carob powder with 2 or 3 drops peppermint oil**
3. **2 or 3 ripe bananas or a mixture of banana and carob powder**
4. **⅓ cup cocoa with ½ cup pecans.**

Dissolve the slippery elm powder in the water. It should mix into a mucilaginous blob. Put it in the blender with ½ cup soy milk and the honey. Blend until smooth. Add the vanilla and sea salt and whatever flavoring you choose. Blend again, add the rest of the soy milk, and mix until smooth. Put into a tray and freeze until almost hard. Put the mixture back into the blender and whip until emulsified. Refreeze and it's ready to eat.

Variation

In the basic recipe (before adding the flavorings), replace 1 cup soy milk with 1 cup coconut milk, and add ½ cup toasted grated coconut and a dash toasted sesame oil.

Honey Chocolate Topping

Try this topping on the vanilla, banana, or coconut variation versions.

2 tablespoons butter or coconut fat
¼ cup honey
2 tablespoons malt syrup
2 squares unsweetened chocolate, melted,
   or ¼ cup carob powder
1 teaspoon vanilla extract
2 teaspoons heavy cream or coconut
   cream (optional)

Melt the butter and blend in the honey and malt syrup in a saucepan over low heat. Stir in the chocolate (or carob powder), blend well, then add the vanilla and cream, if desired. Serve warm. Coconut fat is especially good here because it makes a texture that melts easily at a low temperature, but turns hard when you put it over ice cream.

Preparation time: 15 minutes; 1 to 1 ½ hours to freeze

Carob Fudge Balls

⅓ cup peanut butter
⅓ cup tahini
⅓ to ½ cup honey or malt syrup
½ cup carob powder
2 tablespoons vanilla extract
¼ cup chopped raisins, currants, or dates
⅓ cup chopped nuts
⅓ cup sesame, sunflower seeds
¼ cup coconut, shredded or desiccated
¾ cup toasted wheat germ or toasted
   coconut, for coating

Mix the peanut butter and tahini in a bowl and cream in the honey or malt syrup. Sift the carob powder and stir it in. Add the vanilla. Now stir in all the fruit, nuts, seeds, and coconut, and mix to a fudge-like cohesiveness. Roll into bite-size balls and roll them in the wheat germ to coat.

Chill and eat. Kids like these just as much as candy (they like to roll them too!).

Preparation time: 10-12 minutes; 30 minutes to chill

Tahini Date Treats

2 tablespoons malt syrup
½ cup tahini
⅓ cup flaked coconut
½ teaspoon vanilla extract
12 large dates
12 pecan or walnut halves

Cream the syrup and tahini. Add the coconut, then the vanilla, and mix until blended. Split and pit the dates and fill with a teaspoon of tahini mix, shaping aesthetically. Crown with a pecan half and chill an hour or so.

Preparation time: 8 minutes

Tahini Natto Treats

Here is an exotic sort of candy. They aren't too sweet.

¼ cup natto miso (try to avoid kombu
   strips—little seaweed pieces—while
   spooning out)
½ cup tahini
2 tablespoons honey or malt syrup
¼ cup peanut butter
⅓ cup sesame seeds
Dash toasted sesame oil
⅓ cup toasted wheat germ or toasted
   sesame seeds

Cream the natto with the tahini. Add the honey and peanut butter and cream again. Add the sesame seeds and oil and stir until an even consistency is reached. Roll into balls between your palms and coat with wheat germ or sesame seeds. These will keep in the refrigerator up to a month in an airtight container.

Preparation time: 10 minutes

SESAME BRITTLE

Here's a favorite in the ranks of the down-and-out dessert! It's late, you get an insatiable craving, you go into the kitchen, and there's not a sweet treat on the horizon. Do you go down to the inconvenience store and grab a candy bar off the shelf?

Let me save you a trip (and your adrenals one, too, as that sugar is going to make you feel yucky in the morning). With a little imagination, this recipe and a few ingredients that you can substitute, you can be munching a delightful healthy candy within the half hour.

1 cup sunflower seeds
1 cup sesame seeds
Dash soy sauce (no more than 1 teaspoon)
½ cup melted butter, coconut fat, or sesame, walnut, or peanut oil
½ cup sweetener, honey, malt syrup, maple syrup
1–2 teaspoons vanilla extract

Dry roast the seeds in a skillet. They brown at different rates, so you must do them separately. Also roast any nuts you like or may have on hand—almonds, walnuts, pecans, filberts, cashews, pine nuts—to total 2 cups of seeds and nuts. Put a dash of soy sauce over the seeds or nuts at the last minute. Stir briskly, empty from the pan, and put aside to cool.

Warm the butter and sweetening. Bring to a boil and hold there for 5 or 6 minutes. Cool slightly and add the vanilla. Pour the seeds/nuts into the syrup and mix thoroughly to coat everything. Butter or oil a plate or cookie sheet. Drop the mixture by spoonfuls onto the plate or make a thin layer across the whole sheet (though cutting it to pieces after it's chilled can be quite a hassle). Pop in the fridge until it sets, then crunch away.

This same recipe makes a great pancake topping served warm. You might wish to use somewhat fewer seeds/nuts proportionately.

Preparation time: 12 minutes; 30 minutes to chill

Specialty Cookbooks from The Crossing Press

Biscotti, Brownies, and Bars
By Terri Henry

$6.95 • Paper • ISBN 0-89594-901-6

One-Dish Stove Top Meals
By Jane Marsh Dieckmann

$6.95 • Paper • ISBN 0-89594-968-7

Old World Breads
By Charel Scheele

$6.95 • Paper • ISBN 0-89594-902-4

Pestos! Cooking with Herb Pastes
By Dorothy Rankin

$8.95 • Paper • ISBN 0-89594-180-5

Quick Breads
By Howard Early and Glenda Morris

$6.95 • Paper • ISBN 0-89594-941-5

Salad Dressings
By Teresa H. Burns

$6.95 • Paper • ISBN 0-89594-895-8

Salsas!
By Andrea Chesman

$6.95 • Paper • ISBN 0-89594-178-3

Sauces for Pasta!
By K. Trabant with A. Chesman

$8.95 • Paper • ISBN 0-89594-403-0

Sun-Dried Tomatoes
By Andrea Chesman

$6.95 • Paper • ISBN 0-89594-900-8

Wholesome Cookies
By Jane Marsh Dieckmann

$6.95 • Paper • ISBN 0-89594-942-3

To receive a current catalog from The Crossing Press, please call toll-free, 800-777-1048.
Visit our Website on the Internet at: www.crossingpress.com